The Grid Down Prepper

How to survive when the power goes out

By Robert Paine

© 2014

Are You and Your Family Ready to Survive Without Power?

Are you prepared for when the power grid goes down? There are any number of things that can cause a power grid collapse: war, government interference, natural disasters, and on and on. You can have the greatest prepping plan in the world, but if you forget to prep for a power grid collapse, all of your hard work will be for nothing. So where to start?

You have to start somewhere. You can start with the items in this guide. Inside The Grid Down Prepper, you'll learn:

- What the power grid is, and how we rely on it
- Probable Causes of a Grid Collapse
- What will happen after a Collapse
- How to prepare for limited or no power
- Tips for finding and using water, how to cook, cool, heat, and light your survival
- Much, much more

It isn't all about buying food and supplies. There is a lot of research and planning that goes into prepping for a power grid collapse. That is going to be where your prepping journey starts. Slow and easy is the way to go!

If you are interested in learning how to protect your family from a power grid collapse, this book is your first step to learning how to prepare. Get started today!

Sign up for Robert's Mailing List to be notified of **New Releases** and **Special Sales**: http://eepurl.com/zvm11

What to do when the Power Grid goes down?

Introduction

Have you ever dealt with a power outage? Maybe it lasted for only a few hours or maybe all day. It was probably frustrating, but not that big of a concern because you knew it would be back up soon. What would you do if the power grid went down for an extended period of time? Would you know how to survive? To thrive?

It is almost impossible to think of our lives without electricity. Everything we do is somehow connected to the power grid. Imagine your morning routine for a minute. You get up, probably turn on the radio or television to hear the news for the day. Maybe you go for your phone, which has been charging in the electrical plug-in all night. Turn on the coffee maker before jumping in a hot shower. Before you head out the door, you grab a couple waffles out of the freezer and pop them in the toaster. You go to work, you use computers, the elevator and lights. Do you see where this is going? We, as a society living in a very modern world, are completely reliant upon electricity. We can't eat breakfast, brush our teeth or entertain ourselves without electricity. And most of us don't ever give it a second thought.

Though we may never even think about it, the possibility of the power grid failing is very real. Choosing to put your head in the sand and ignore all of the warning signs isn't helpful. Just because we are used to something and it seems like it has always been there, we cannot ignore the fact that the possibility exists. The government knows the power grid can and likely will fail at some point. They run drills with law enforcement, EMS and even the military on how to handle such a situation. Many people don't fully understand how widespread a power grid failure would be.

Minor power outages tend to affect only certain parts of the city, one or two blocks, leaving some stores open for business. Most people, therefore, see these as small inconveniences, tiny little blips in an otherwise perfectly-working system. But that is simply not the case! If the power grid goes down, nothing about our daily lives would be "normal". Things would not just continue to go along, as if nothing had happened. A major grid failure would paralyze an entire region, effecting hundreds of thousands, possibly millions of people. If the entire U.S. system goes down – well, you can start to imagine the chaos and mayhem an event of that size would cause.

Everything we do involves electricity. It touches nearly every aspect of our modern world. And it's not just contained to our lives at home or inside buildings. Think outside the four walls of your home for a minute. Check out some of the things from the following list and then you will see just how serious a power grid failure would be.

- Gas pumps wouldn't work

- Cash registers wouldn't work and safes wouldn't be able to be opened

- Credit card machines wouldn't work

- ATM machines would be down

- Banks would be shut down

- Grocery stores would be unable to sell you food

- Businesses without backup generators would close—those that had generators will only have the gas on hand to run the generators

- Traffic lights would stop

- Subways and rail systems would stop

- Restaurants would be unable to cook or serve food

- Hospitals and clinics would not have access to electronic patient records, which would make healthcare a serious concern

And that's just a start. This is why a power grid failure would be devastating. Commerce would be halted, which means you wouldn't be able to work and earn a paycheck. The money you have on hand when the power grid fails is all you have to get by on. The modern world, as we know it, would grind to a halt. It is a serious situation that deserves attention. Even some of the most-seasoned preppers only prepare for one event, say, a governmental collapse or a natural disaster. A power grid failure is often one of the least-prepared for events. But now that you know how serious it can get, you can start working on a plan. Preparing to ride out a grid failure is your best hope. If you are prepared to survive, and thrive, without electricity, you will be better off than 99.9% of the population. And that's what it's all about – being prepared!

So, let's get started.

Possible Causes of the Grid going down

Believe it or not, there are actually several different reasons the power grid could fail. It would be easier to believe that it couldn't happen if there was only a single, far-fetched reason. Unfortunately, there are plenty of very real scenarios that could leave us all sitting in the dark for days, weeks and possibly even months. The following are some of the most likely causes of a grid failure, though they are, for sure, not the only possibilities.

Natural disaster

This one is not hard to believe for most people, when you really start to talk to them about the grid going down. Many people have even experienced it themselves, on much smaller levels. Natural disasters are a common occurrence these days. Things like hurricanes, tornadoes, blizzards, and earthquakes can easily take out a power grid. We have seen it happen several times in the past couple of years, all over the United States and Europe. A severe storm or extremely strong weather is always a possibility. Depending on the severity of the disaster and the area that was hit, a power outage could affect millions of people.

Remember when New Orleans was left in the dark for days? Or, more recently, we saw Hurricane Sandy cripple New York City. Do you remember how people responded to such weather events? They panicked. They didn't know what to do. People were forced into darkness for several days. In the hours and days before Sandy hit, stores were wiped out of things like water, bread and flashlights.

Even those minor preps did very little to help those who were left without power for several weeks. And this was with advanced warning!

Things like earthquakes, on the other hand, give no warning. We know certain areas are due for a strong earthquake, but nobody knows when it will strike. Can you imagine the chaos and panic that would ensue if a major earthquake hits San Francisco again (like it is predicted to)? If people have a hard time prepping and surviving with advanced warnings even, then they have no hope of making it through an unplanned, unannounced natural disaster such as an earthquake.

War (foreign or domestic)

We have been very fortunate not to have a foreign war on our soil in the past couple hundred years. Yes, we have had terrorist attacks. However, those are typical fairly localized and do not disrupt the grid in any meaningful way. Many of us would not be prepared for an invasion by a foreign army or a terrorist attack on the national power grid. If a bomb was dropped that took out a power grid, we would suffer greatly. In fact, a small nuclear bomb detonated way above the atmosphere, it would create an electromagnetic pulse that would paralyze the power grid. The nuclear fallout would be nothing compared to the failed power grid.

It doesn't only have to be an attack from a foreign government. There are plenty of folks right here in the country who are willing to make war or who are actively trying to disrupt our daily lives. Many are predicting we are headed for another civil war of sorts. If that happens, the power grid would be at risk. It would likely be one of the first things targeted because it would result in so much damage.

In the event of a war or a terrorist attack on the power grid system, who knows how long it would take to get back to 'normal'. The government and armed forces will be busy trying to take care of the immediate armed threat. Average citizens will be at home, scared to death. Who will fix the power grid? How long will it take? We have no way of knowing, so the only thing we can is prepare to live without electricity for as long as it may take.

Terrorism (foreign or domestic)

An act of terror doesn't always come in the form of a bomb or some other equally horrible attack. A single computer virus that was programmed to take out our power grid is a real possibility. There have been plenty of rumors this type of attack is imminent. The attack could come from the outside or on our own soil. Recently, several power stations in California were shot out. The power company was able to divert power to other transformers and prevent a widespread outage, but many are concerned this one attack was a dry run. If there was a coordinated attack on a dozen or more stations throughout an area, it would cause widespread power outages. It would take weeks for the power company to repair the transformers and restore power. That is assuming the rest of the power grid did not come under attack.

Action by our government or outside players

Our government may choose to shut down portions of the power grid for numerous reasons. If there is civil unrest and rioting that is causing serious damage, the government may opt to cut the power to an area until order can be restored. We've seen this tactic used in isolated neighborhoods already, but it could just as easily be used in entire cities, regions, even states. Military Law could be imposed that would limit the amount of power delivered to a particular area. If power was in short supply due to a natural disaster, act of war, or simply because the grid is overtaxed, the government could choose to limit power and divert it as they see fit.

We've already seen rolling blackouts in parts of the country, so it's not too far-fetched to imagine the government trying this technique across the entire country, in greater and greater time periods, leaving us with no choice but to try and survive without electricity until they decide to restore it for us. That is a situation we are prepping to avoid – we want to be able to survive and thrive without electricity and to not be dependent on the government, or anyone else.

Experts agree that our power infrastructure is extremely vulnerable to a cyber or physical attack. We've seen cyber terrorists and hackers already easily steal personal data from hundreds of thousands of Americans through coordinated online attacks. It's not a big stretch to see them attack another portion of the U.S. through online attacks. Many of the power grids across America are extremely old and outdated. They might have little to no digital security and may be particularly vulnerable to cyber attacks. The government recognizes this vulnerability and has been working behind the scenes to prepare for the ultimate take down of the grid. Communications during a grid failure will be restricted, so the government is coordinating their reaction with several agencies in order to institute protocol if and when the grid fails.

What may happen if the Grid Collapses

Now that you see just how possible it is for the grid to collapse, let's get into what could actually happen in the midst of the grid collapse. As we discussed earlier, our entire lives center around electricity. If you don't have a car charger for your cell phone, laptop or tablet, it won't be long before those are rendered useless. Sitting in a dark, quiet house for a couple hours is nothing compared to going days on end with no electricity. It's not something that most of us are used to. If you are unable to work and the kids can't go to school, it won't be long before you start climbing the walls! We have become so accustomed to being plugged in that we struggle to get through the day without using our favorite appliances and devices. When people are unplugged with no warning, they are going to struggle and tensions are going to rise quickly.

The average person or family will be completely lost with the most mundane tasks, such as how to eat, bathe and even keep themselves and their surroundings safe and clean. Your hot water tank would be useless. Most people wouldn't know how to start a fire to cook with and would be forced to eat cold goods or boxed items like crackers and cookies. Washing your hands would have to be done with cold water because you couldn't even heat water on the stove. Think back again to Hurricane Katrina and Hurricane Sandy. These events first took the country by surprise. Yes, people knew the storms were coming, but even then they were not prepared to deal with a failed power grid and the destruction of the hurricane-force winds. With Hurricane Sandy, New York knew it was coming at least a week in advance and most people thought they were prepared, with families buying a couple loaves of bread and a pack of batteries for their flashlights. They were in for a big, nasty surprise when the storm left many areas of the city in the dark for days. We saw how much chaos and havoc that caused. Now imagine that on a larger, national scale.

After these big storms, we saw that it wasn't long before people were out of food, batteries and clean drinking water. The 3-day supply the government recommends is typically not enough and those people learned that the hard way. Some people were prepared with canned food and freeze-dried packs of food. Did they remember to factor in the extra water needed to rehydrate the food or a manual can opener to open the canned food?

Most people would be completely thrown off of their normal lives if the power were to go down for an extended period of time. Kids would likely suffer the worst. They have been brought up in a technical age where most of their toys are powered by electricity or batteries. They are used to watching television and playing video games. Adults are used to being able to surf the Internet while watching television. It can leave a person feeling a little lost when their routines are severely interrupted. You would seriously stand in your kitchen and feel like you were in a foreign land. No microwave, no stove and no refrigerator. Whatever was in your pantry would be what you had for dinner. You couldn't run through the drive-thru anywhere or go out to eat because you don't have power at home. They wouldn't have power either. So, what would you do?

The upheaval in typical routine would leave many people struggling to the point they would do things they wouldn't normally do. If a person was left in the dark without any food, water, or a way to light their home, they may resort to looting store shelves. Imagine if the kids are crying and begging you for food. You would do just about anything to take care of your family. People figure if others are looting the stores, you jumping in and grabbing a few supplies won't make a difference. We can see how this would quickly get out of control.

Lawlessness would make the streets unsafe. That means people would be forced to hole up in their homes and wait for help. Again, refer back to the chaos following Hurricane Katrina. The city of New Orleans was nearly destroyed by the looting and destructing by disgruntled citizens. Sure, the hurricane caused plenty of damage, but it was the days following the storm that made it unsafe to be outside. Can you imagine this happening in your town? If not, you should. It can, and may, happen in any town across the United States. So, how can you prepare?

How to prepare for limited access to running water

One of the biggest concerns you should have following a collapse of the power grid is water. Obviously, we all need water to survive. It's the most important thing we need to secure. Yet, for most people, water security means buying a case of bottled water and calling it a day. This isn't good enough!

When the grid goes down, your tap water would no longer be safe to drink. Without a filtering system at the water sanitation department, the water coming through your tap would be unclean and, oftentimes, harmful to drink. Eventually, the water would dry up without pumps to pump it to your home. Stores will run out of bottled water quickly as panic sets in and people rush out to buy up as much water as they can.

You need to be ahead of this rush. You need water to survive. That is a given. In fact, you need at least a gallon of water per day for each member of your family. If you have pets, factor in another gallon of water. You cannot live more than a couple of days without water. Expert survivalists put the magic number as 3 days, but you would be feeling pretty rotten by day two without water.

You must be prepared to take care of your water situation immediately following the power grid failing. If you happen to be home, fill your bathtub with water, fill every available pot with water and disconnect the water heater. The water in the tank will be a backup supply, but you don't want contaminated water from the outside coming in. You will have a good supply to start with, but you need to be prepared to restock your water supply, and to do so quickly.

How to Find Water

If you don't have enough water stored in your home, you are going to need to track some down. Stores will be crazy with mad rushes of people looking to buy every last bottle of water. You'll want to avoid that madness. One way you can prepare for this eventuality is by getting a map or taking a walk or drive today to find the closest body of water. Do some scouting of your nearby surroundings and find one or two streams, rivers, or lakes. Walking the route is a good idea so you can get familiar with the path and learn how long it takes you to make it to the water. Again, lakes, streams, rivers and ponds are all options, so keep an eye out for any of them. Yes, pond water may seem nasty, but you can drink it in a pinch after purifying it, which we will discuss in the next section.

If you have bugged out to a second location after a grid collapse, you may not be as familiar with the area. In this case, one of the easiest ways to spot water is look for lots of green vegetation. Green signifies water is somewhere nearby. You can also look for animal tracks or look for birds flying over an area. The animals will lead you to water. Bees also tend to fly towards water. Certain trees are indicators of a steady supply of water as well. Cypress, water oak and river birch will only grow near water.

If you are in an arid area, you can dig, but this should only be done if you know that the water is relatively close to the surface.

Digging is a huge tax on your energy and uses a lot of calories. If you are already on the edge of dehydration, digging with little hope of finding water can be dangerous.

Once you have found a source of water, mark it on your maps. Make sure everyone in your family or surviving party knows where the water source is, and where a backup water source is. Before any major event happens, spend a few weekends practicing how you will get to your water sources. Take turns with different members of your family or party leading the way, so that you make sure everyone knows what to do when the real event happens.

How to Disinfect/Purify Water

Once you have found your water, DON'T DRINK IT! It will be difficult to resist taking just a little sip as you transport your water back home, but you absolutely must not drink it until you know it's safe. You must assume that any water you collect is unsafe to drink. Consider the number of animals that are drinking from the same water source. Animals like to stand in the water when they are drinking and when nature calls, they do their business in that water. Humans are not immune from this either. Water in the open usually contains a variety of dangerous bacteria and viruses that can make a human incredibly sick. The viruses are in the fecal matter of humans and animals and contaminate the water supply. Things like ecoli and giardia can wreak havoc on your digestive system resulting in dehydration or even death. You simply cannot risk drinking water without purifying it.

So how do you ensure the water is safe to drink? The easiest option is to use purification tablets. You will want to load up on several bottles of these. They are typically sold 30 to a bottle. Each tablet will usually purify a quart of water. You need a gallon of water per day per person, so that means a minimum of 4 tablets a day. Stock up on these now. They have a fairly long shelf life, so you can feel comfortable buying as many as you think you'll need. And then, buy a few more. This is one thing you can never have too many of.

Another option for purifying water is to boil it, but this could prove problematic in a world without electricity. If you can build a fire (which you should learn how to do!), then you can simply boil the water over a fire. This is a long-term, sustainable solution and, maybe not unsurprisingly, a skill that 99% of the population does not have. So if you can start a fire and boil your water, you'll be way ahead of the game.

The water only needs to boil a maximum of three minutes. Technically, the first bubble will kill all the microorganisms. Letting it boil longer is a waste of fuel and water lost by evaporation. Adding a few drops of standard household bleach is an option. It is very inexpensive and you only need a 1/4 teaspoon to purify a gallon of water. If the water is particularly cloudy, you may want to increase that to a 1/2 teaspoon. Keep in mind that household bleach has a shelf life of about 6 months before it starts to lose potency.

How to Filter Water

Filtering water is an option, but it is important to note that there are great differences in filters. You need to pay a little more and buy a filter with a .10 micron level of filtering. This is the smallest pore possible and will remove a majority of viruses. If you're relying on filters for your water, you need to get the smallest pores possible.

However, filters shouldn't be used as the only means of cleaning your drinking water. It is best to purify your water and then filter it to make it taste better. In a pinch, you could rely on your filter alone, but it is far from an ideal solution. Run the water through the filter several times to try and get rid of as many microorganisms as possible. If you don't have an actual filter, charcoal from a fire could also be used in combination with rocks and leaves. This is another last-resort type of filtration system, but it is certainly better than not filtering at all.

How to Store Water

You could save yourself a lot of trouble by storing water to drink in case of a grid failure. This will eliminate the need to purify your water or go out searching for it when it could be dangerous to do so. The most obvious choice for storing water is by buying cases of bottled water. This is great for a short-term grid failure situation, but for long-term, it wouldn't be feasible or very affordable. You would have to store about 1.5 cases per day for a family of 4. Assume your power is out for a week and you would need about 11 cases of bottled water. It is a bit of a space and money hog, and not really sustainable for any long-term planning situations.

Another option is to buy a few of the 5-gallon containers. These are made of a sturdy plastic and will store for years. They can be a bit bulky and heavy, so they are not easy to transport or to take with you if you need to bug out. But they can be a nice option if you know you are staying put.

If you have the space at home, look into buying a small water wall. These are square containers that are designed to stack on top of each other. Each container has a spout that makes it easy for you to get a small drink of water. These are a bit easier to store, as they save some space, and with the spout, they are much easier for everyone in the family to learn to use, young and old.

Another option that many people often don't think about is to bottle your own water. However, DO NOT use old milk jugs. The plastic is flimsy and it will break down in a matter of months. Juice containers and 2-liter soda bottles will work. Fill the water from your tap and add a drop of bleach. You will need to rotate your own bottled water supply about every six months, to ensure you have fresh, drinkable water when you need it. If the power goes out and you have "old" water on hand, you could purify it with more bleach or purification tablets to make it safe to drink.

Another idea is to consider investing in rain barrels that are set outside your home. You can store 50 gallons of water in a single barrel and the water is free. You can make your own barrel or buy one at Home Depot. You, of course, have to keep an eye out to ensure that nothing else gets in your barrel and the water is maintained in a safe, clean environment. But if you have the land

and you live in an area of the country that gets enough rain precipitation, rain barrels are a really great solution to water storage.

Sanitation

Staying clean and sanitary in a grid down situation will be a challenge. It's not something that most people think about, but in a long-term survival situation, sanitation can mean the difference between life and death. You can't afford to get sick due to improper sanitation. It is of the utmost importance you keep your home and body free of excess bacteria and germs. When the water isn't running and the toilets aren't flushing, it is a recipe for disaster. Years ago, when a city was left without water, people took to using the bathroom outside and the streets were lined with human fecal matter. It isn't just gross, it is deadly. There are far too many viruses passed through contact with fecal matter. So if you don't pay close attention to sanitation, you're just inviting yourself and your family to get sick and to spread the disease amongst each other. We need to avoid this! So, how to keep clean?

Toilets/Latrines

This may not be your favorite subject, and certainly your children or spouse may not want to think or talk about it, but you are going to have to come up with a way to use the toilet without contaminating your house or yard. There are a few options you have. What you choose to go with will depend on where you live and the weather.

Digging holes is one way to make sure you are taking care of business in a way that won't make anybody sick or stink up the area. It's probably the oldest sanitation method in the book, but it still works to this day, when done correctly. First, simply dig a hole, about six inches deep and do your deed. Fill the hole in. If you are in an area where animals are running around, put a rock or log over the area. You don't want them digging it up. If you have several people in the home, you can dig a bigger trench. Each time somebody uses the bathroom, fill in that section with dirt, working your way down the trench. It's not pleasant, but it will keep all the waste in one location, and covered, which is important.

If going outside isn't really an option, due to weather, or you live in an urban area, or for any other reason, you could line a 5-gallon bucket with a heavy-duty trash bag. A lid will help reduce the odor in between uses. Don't let the bag get overly full. It is a very good idea to double line the bucket. When you need to empty the bucket, take it as far from your home or any areas where people are as possible. Carry the entire bucket outside. Tie the bag off and bury it, if possible. If you don't have a bucket, you could use garbage bags and do the same thing. It's not pretty, but keeping yourself and your living space sanitary is the primary concern.

One more tip: If you are using the bathroom outside, make sure you are at least 200 feet from any water source. You don't want to contaminate the water!

Hand Washing

You need to do your best to wash your hands after using the bathroom, handling garbage or working outside. Of course, you should always be doing this, but in a grid down event, it's going to be even more necessary! Good hand washing will help prevent germs that could make you incredibly ill at a time you really can't afford it. It will also stop germs from spreading amongst your family or anyone else you are surviving with.

While you probably won't have hot water, you can still make do. Put the soap on your hands and work it in. Pour water over your hands to rinse the soap off. Don't use a universal bowl for everybody to wash their hands in. This is just putting all the germs, viruses and bacteria into one place. Do not reuse the water that you run over your hands. Use hand sanitizer after washing and in between washings to try and keep your hands as clean as possible. This is something you can stock up on early, as it has a very long shelf life. Get into the habit of washing hands or using sanitizer after using the restroom, before and after cooking and eating, after venturing outside, and similar situations. This will be an important habit for you and your family to carry on after a grid down event.

Dishes/Clothes

If you don't have disposable cutlery and dishes on hand, you are going to need to wash your dishes after each use. Of course, if you can find ways to eat without having to use dishes, that is equally as desirable. You must use potable water or water that has been purified at least. Don't use the water from the river or stream or pond. Again, those viruses and bacteria will cling to your dishes and end up making you sick. Even after washing, you would be left with bacteria from the dirty water, so it's not worth the risk. Without hot water, it is going to be tough to clean some dishes. Take advantage of soaking to loosen up stubborn messes. Fill the sink halfway with purified water and wash your dishes. Fill the other sink with just enough water to cover a few dishes. You must conserve water while ensuring your dishes are clean.

Your clothing will need to be as clean as possible to ensure you are not making your body dirty. If you are going to be working outside in the garden or doing something that you know will make you dirty, have a set of clothes set aside purely for those tasks. Put on the dirty clothes to do the work and then bathe and put on clean clothes. You will need to wash clothes by hand. A washing board is great, but if you don't have one (few people do) you can do without. It may not get your clothes as clean as your Maytag, but it will do. Air-dry the clothes either outside or in the house. They will dry, eventually. Develop these habits for yourself and your family now, so that when a grid down event happens, cleanliness will be second nature for you all.

Personal Hygiene

Taking a hot shower in the morning is going to be a bit difficult in a grid down situation. However, you can still maintain basic hygiene. You will want to. No, you will *need* to. You are likely going to be in close quarters with the family and doing more manual labor than you are accustomed to. That means sweating, which can get real stinky, real quick. Daily sponge baths that focus on the problem areas are important. It doesn't take much water to take a quick sponge bath. Start at the top and work your way down.

You could also invest in something known as a camp shower. These lovely tools hold about three gallons water. You place the bag in the sun to heat the water. A nozzle hangs down and gives you a nice spray of warm water. The showers are very inexpensive and a worthy investment for those who want to prepare for a grid failure. Conserve water by getting wet, turn off the water, lather up and then rinse. You can easily take a nice, cleansing shower with two gallons of water. Cleanliness will help evade sickness, will lift your spirits, and will make everyone around you happier.

Cooking/Cooling/Lighting/Heating

When you are holed up in your home with your family, you need to do what you can to keep everybody comfortable. This means cool or warm temps, depending on the season, full bellies, and staying out of the dark as much as possible. This is going to be one of your most challenging tasks. Let's address each one of these issues separately, in order to make it easier to digest.

Cooking

You cannot live on canned beans alone. It would make you ill and very irritable. You will want to build up a nice food storage that will give you some variety. You should be doing this already, if you are prepping at all, so storing food for a grid down scenario will be no different than any other survival situation. Focus on foods with long shelf lives, that pack great nutrition punches into the smallest sizes possible, and make sure to have some variety so that you and your family don't lose your minds eating the same over and over. There are a few options you have to heating up your meals or actually cooking a meal.

• Solar ovens are handy tools you can use whether you have electricity or not. They are a lot like a crackpot. The ovens rely on the sun's rays to heat the box and cook the food inside. You can make your own solar oven out of a cardboard box, tin foil and heavy plastic sheeting. The foil lining will reflect the sun's rays and the plastic sheeting will keep the heat in. You can cook meat, casseroles, breads and so on in your solar oven.

• An open fire is also an option if you have a fire pit or capability to make one. You can use cast iron cookware to cook over the fire. You can also wrap food in tin foil and place it on the hot coals around the edge of the fire. This is one way to make bread, cook potatoes or even a stew inside the foil. Load up on tin foil for your prepping pantry and make sure you and at least one other person are well-versed in starting fires in a variety of situations.

• Coleman stoves are a favorite, but in order to use your stove, you need plenty of propane canisters. There are various opinions about using a propane stove indoors. Technically, you shouldn't. It's a safety hazard. If you can, it's always preferable to cook your meals on the back porch or outside. If inside is the absolute only place you can cook, due to safety, weather, etc., make sure you do it in a well-ventilated room, as far from anything flammable as possible, and take all the necessary safety precautions.

• The barbecue on the back deck is an option. Consider investing in a portable barbecue that uses briquettes and stock up on them. Propane will likely not be available immediately following the failed power grid.

• Sterno cans are another option for heating a can of food or water to use to rehydrate a freeze-dried meal pack. You would need quite a few of these cans if it is more than just you and you are going to be without power for a while.

• If the power failure happens in winter and you have a wood stove you use for heat, you have a cook top right there! You can heat water, cook eggs and even bake a pie on top of your wood stove.

Cooling

If the power goes out in the middle of the summer and the temperatures are skyrocketing, you need to be able to retreat to somewhere cool. If you have plenty of shade trees around your house, you can keep your home fairly comfortable. If you are exposed, you may be better off getting outside and into some shade, as it will often be cooler outdoors in the shade, than inside in a hot, stuffy house.

Keep your house cool by shutting the doors and windows as soon as the temperature starts to warm up. Cover the windows with heavy curtains or blankets to block the sun – you'd be amazed how much just sunlight through a window can heat up a room until it becomes uncomfortable. Open the windows at night to take advantage of the cooler temperatures outside. Dress in cooler clothing. Lightweight fabrics are best and will lift your moods considerably. You can help cool your body temperature by dipping a washcloth or old t-shirt into water and placing it on the back of your neck.

Save the majority of your chores for early morning or late evening when it is coolest out. Hang out in the basement or in the northeast corner of your home that will get the least amount of sun and will therefore be cooler. You can also invest in a solar-powered fan that can create a nice breeze.

Lighting

Although light isn't a necessity to survive, it sure does make you feel better and does make you feel safer. For that reason alone, it's worth taking a look at how you can keep your family in light. You don't have to worry about tripping over stuff and hurting yourself. Your children will feel much safer and happier in light.

Flashlights are great, but do you have enough batteries? LED flashlights are extra great because they are super bright and use very little battery power. Thus, they last for a long time before you have to change batteries, unlike more traditional flashlights. Look into getting a solar-powered lantern or a crank radio/flashlight even. The lantern will be bright enough to light an entire room. This will save you from relying on batteries. Save the flashlight for when you need to run outside to use the bathroom or for more emergency-type of situations.

Another idea is to stock up on emergency candles. These are designed to burn much brighter than the typical scented candles you find at the store. Don't forget candleholders. Spend a few nights with your spouse or children practicing with living by candlelight. This can be a fun activity for the family and in the event of a grid down situation, everyone will feel much more comfortable with the whole idea and practice of living by candlelight at night.

Heating

If the power failure happens during the winter, you need to be able to stay warm. A wood stove is your best option in most climates and situations. Make sure you have plenty of seasoned firewood on hand to burn. It's a good idea to get a wood stove now, if possible, so you can start practicing. It's not that easy to find suitable wood, learn how to chop that wood properly, then learn how to store it properly, and finally, learn how to burn it properly. These are all skills that take time, so the sooner you start learning, the better.

If you don't have a wood stove, pick the smallest room in your house and keep everyone inside. Huddle together with blankets. Body heat will help keep you warm. Much warm than people often realize, in fact. Cover the windows with heavy blankets to block cold air from coming in. If you have a south-facing window, leave it uncovered to take advantage of the heat from the sun. Cover it at night or if the sun is blocked. Dress in several layers. Wear a warm hat. Your body heat escapes through your head. Build a fort out of blankets or set up you tent in the living room. The small space will help trap the heat and will keep you warm.

Many people will have a generator at home. They think that if the power goes out, they'll just turn the generator on and then life will continue like normal. This is a big mistake – especially if the grid goes down in the dead of winter. If you plan on running a generator night and day, that's going to use up an awful lot of gasoline. How much gasoline do you have in storage? Probably not a lot. If you think it will be easy to just rush out and buy some gasoline for your generator when you run out, think again.

It's fine to have a generator and to be prepared to use it, but you'd better have a backup plan for when your generator runs out of gasoline or, worse, breaks completely. You don't want to be unprepared when that eventually happens – and it will!

Conclusion

There are any number of reasons why the power grid might go down. Natural disasters. War. Terrorism. Economic collapse. Governmental action. And on and on. We can't control any of those situations. What we *can* control is how well prepared we will be for them and how we will respond to them. That is the essence of prepping, and prepping for a power grid failure is no different. Yet, for some reason, this seems to be one area of prepping that most folks seem to ignore. Many people plan for wars, government overthrows, extreme weather or, if they're really out there, crazy things like zombie attacks. They don't stop and consider what is one of the most likely causes of a survival scenario: a complete collapse of the power grid and days, months, or even years without electricity. Don't be one of them!

Living without electricity can seem daunting, but if you are prepared, you will get by just fine. You may even learn to appreciate some of the little things in life. You will certainly forge closer bonds with your family members when the technological distractions are removed from your lives. You will learn valuable skills like cooking from scratch and how to build a fire. You would be best served to learn these skill before the grid fails. Talk to your family about what life will be like without power. Do your best to reassure them that you are preparing to ride out the grid failure and they don't have to panic.

Make it an adventure! Learn some camp songs to sing as you sit around your living room in the evening. When you take the time to prepare today, by doing things like storing extra food, water and maybe even collecting extra blankets to add to your linen closet, you are ensuring your family will be taken care of despite the dark world they have been thrust into.

We have seen towns, cities, and even entire states, thrust into chaos following failures of the power grid. Riots, looting, lines at stores and gas stations, and confusion is not uncommon in these situations. Why? Simply because the vast majority of Americans are completely unprepared to live without electricity. It's not something they've ever thought of, and certainly have never practiced or prepared for.

But you are different. You are thinking about it already. You are preparing. You are taking the necessary steps to secure your future and the safety of your family and loved ones. Stay on that path and nothing but good things will come.

Good luck, fellow Preppers!

*****

If you've enjoyed this book, **please** consider leaving a review and letting others know what you thought!

Sign up for Robert's Mailing List to be notified of **New Releases** and **Special Sales**: http://eepurl.com/zvm11

No Spam – he promises!

Other Books by Robert Paine:
Prepper's Pantry: A Survival Food Guide
The Survivalist Cookbook - Recipes for Preppers
Prepping 101: A Beginner's Survival Guide
The Dead Road: The Complete Collection

www.ingramcontent.com/pod-product-compliance
Lightning Source LLC
Chambersburg PA
CBHW070524290526
45790CB00003B/1283